FLUDDE

SARABANDE BOOKS
Louisville, KY

PETER MISHLER

Library of Congress Cataloging-in-Publication Data
Names: Mishler, Peter, author.
Title: Fludde : poems / by Peter Mishler.
Description: First edition. | Louisville, KY : Sarabande Books, 2018
Identifiers: LCCN 2017033118 (print) | LCCN 2017045204 (ebook)
ISBN 9781946448101 (ebook) | ISBN 9781946448194 (softcover : acid-free paper)
Classification: LCC PS3613.I8443 (ebook) | LCC PS3613.I8443 A6 2018 (print)
DDC 811/.6—dc23
LC record available at https://lccn.loc.gov/ 2017033118

Cover design by Kristen Radtke.
Interior by Alban Fischer.
Manufactured in Canada.
This book is printed on acid-free paper.
Sarabande Books is a nonprofit literary organization.

  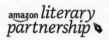

This project is supported in part by an award from the National Endowment for the Arts.
The Kentucky Arts Council, the state arts agency, supports Sarabande Books with state
tax dollars and federal funding from the National Endowment for the Arts.

TO MY WIFE AND DAUGHTER

CONTENTS

FOREWORD

Occasionally, poetry provides us with raw proof of what it is
to be alive, perceptions that never stray far from sensations,
an illumination of sparks as opposed to, or at least in addition
to, the steady artificial light of reason. The poems in *Fludde* are
tributes to the imagination's ability to see through the tissues
of the ordinary to something far more disruptive and timeless.
They exhibit our blown-apart mythologies, persuading us that
the occupations, diversions, and ailments of the world as it is
presented to us, that we are trapped in, can't be all there is. "In
the shed, I hear/the thinning crows/stringing together/a final
crown/of rebar for my head." Such is the view of our corona-
tions: unlikely, maybe even silly.

Fludde reminds us vulnerability is a precursor for transfor-
mation. I feel something in them I always trust: the deploy-
ment of form, musicality, narrative, and wild association,
permitting the reader to see beyond the life of a single poet,
and outside our current moment. The poems are not cut-up
essays. They are not political diatribes. They know what Lorca
knew: there's a drop of duck's blood under every skyscraper.
And what Harold Lloyd knew: that we are all hanging from
a minute hand. Or Andre Breton or Paul Eluard: that we are

prisoners of raindrops. Full of the feral joy of invention and profoundly animated, *Fludde* makes us feel, as only poetry can, that we've found a companion for our dream life. I'd say this is good news.

—Dean Young, 2016

FLUDDE

OLD WORLD

I am collecting insects
from the ground
before the water table
turns on us again.
I am breathing in
the bread of the living
though my little ghosts
are in tune with what I take.
Let me not deceive you
first flowers of sacrilege:
I won't go bawling
from the labyrinth,
my rashes and sores
handled wrongly.
The physician may rest
in his mountain.
The wefts and warps
of the globe may rest.
My love with her tongue
at the tip of the truncheon.
Me with my tongue

asleep at her hipbone.
A field of horses
disperse before
the revelling places
for monsters.
Let the beleaguered
return to their safes.
Let the dying
be returned to the sea.
Our failed hobbies burnt
in the rites of idiots.
Our carted rubble sits
in its fine anterior rage.

SUBLUNARY LIFE

The boy scouts lined up on the freezing banks
about to recite their summerland cheer.
In your bath it trickled down from your scalp
to your golden neck. The parts of me
that could see this were always blundering.
I laid them to rest in the heather
beside a half row of blue city shuttles.
They comfortably watch the semaphores
braiding the sky with silvery aircrafts
above the disengaged shallows. A dish
of its waters need not be drawn up for you.
Our bodies grew smaller when we made love
in the microtel. Ice formed on the walls.
Where are those pearly tenements now?
I brought my shoulders before their windows.
Shadows like lozenges hummed down the moat.
The water-warped doorways thrummed with the past,
and two famously lonely children beneath them
were shading in bar graphs to measure our seasons.

PATERNITY TEST

Child with the gleam
of alimentum
on his chin,
he leads you quickly
past the paintings
in the hall,
a row of still lifes
of a hoof
detached from its animal
in various lights.
Now, he gestures,
you may walk before him.
The sensation
of bearing death
upon your back
across the river.
It is evening there,
and you wear
the flowing robes
of an indeterminate
lunar dye.

4

From where is the smell
of wisteria
burnt abruptly
in a corporate tower?
On the opposite shore . . .
no, no, it is here,
here in these scented candles
at the end of the hall.
The child resumes his lead.
A chair, a table,
a place setting before you.
Fresh-cut flowers.
On a flatscreen,
the Spice Channel
warbles overhead,
its picture scrambling
from pink to green
to black,
and back again.
It's on low,
explains the child,
but this can be changed,
the monitor twisting
on its rope
above you.
The first course
is presented.
You detect a trembling

in the child's hands.
It is his cough
served on a segment
of a wooden balustrade.
He lays it carefully
across your plate.
He lowers his head.
The cough is crystallized
and sweet,
and it calls to you
as faintly
as the imperceptible
chain-tug
of the tilt of the Earth.
It's yours.

WORKHORSE

When I was young they scored me
and buried their straw in me
and let whatever gold clot in me
invested in me and scared my old life
out of me the way they said
it was meant. I played on the floors
of their waiting rooms by the doors
to my first physicians and when
the worst possible faces emerged
I answered all of their questions
as if I were calling into a canyon.
Surely this could not be the present
from which I would flee, the earth
collapsing to fill up a song in their heads.
But I would not chauffeur it for them
so they buckled my knees for me
while I flinched at the cold, scaly walls
of their offices. Their children basked
with their sunlit hands on their cleft
handlebars at the edge of the track.
I lay down in the ruts of their wheels.

They had me design my stable myself
and design it dutifully. They told me
that no one would clean my own pen
and I wouldn't and wouldn't permit myself
not to dream of such strange animals running
to drink from a dish in a far-off clearing.

FROM THE INCORPORATED LIMITS

The freeway rumbles
the mulch at nightfall.
Black leaves trundle
under the earth in silence.
I hear their suffocating.
This is the thoroughfare
of the child: her bedsheet
crowning her shoulders,
she's led by the coughing
of oars on water,
her friends all gathered
to cut and strip
the bark from the birches
for bracelets, for cuffs.
The self-appointed
countess of them whines,
betrayed as she is
by her land and her people.
Her wrists are wilting
in fetters of wood.
Low-pitched and dampened,

a canal-song unfolds.
In concrete, a pattern
of flames on the levee wall.
Over the water, the voices
of children announcing
another kingdom allayed.

SALVATION ARMY

Officer,
now that you've parted
the noble gasses of heaven,
evaded the worm
who feeds
on our first green selves,
you are finished
with keeping the peace,
collecting its taxes,
done with the telexes
crossing your desk,
your children's memories
broadcast
twenty-four hours a day
atop the militia towers.
Done with the upper-
echelon malls,
the sylvan suburbs,
the salted fields.
Tonight,
the embassy garden

is thronged for you
with freckled girls,
a hospital bed
of innumerable threadcount,
and palm
after dew-blighted palm.
You flip your pocket change
onto the boots
of the pockmarked
lyrist from Thrace,
and he plays
and he plays for you,
and he dumbs down the sound
of your aircraft
dropping new tennis shoes
into the mountains.

MILD INVECTIVE

I'm embarrassed.
Four deer step
onto the embankment
beside the Sunoco
at dawn, champing
and misting their breath.
And I'm shaving in my car
which doesn't matter.
The deer have their luxuries
I can't condemn,
and the elderly
fly their small crafts
above us, with cancer
and in love.
I feel I must become
religious for a time
as each new vision
is projected
from my mouth.
This isn't jealousy.
I'm concerned:

it must stand for me
that the outright
and bright-lit places
are plainly unanswerable.

A ROMANCE

I doubled at the waist before a well
to drain the water from the stalk
of my fake flower,
then collapsed onto a cart of wood
the woodsman hauled away.
We passed below the miles of trees.
I heard the fine abrasions
of his coat against his axe,
my colored scarves still spilling
from a marbled suitcase
in my rented room.
His cart, I braved it like a bed,
my underfeathers festering and blue,
my forehead falling
toward my chin at eventide,
the evening falling
on my eyelids when I blinked.
The starlight cooled.
I felt its stellar wind blow through me
as I gathered on my chest
its bright deposits

which I kept
to build my inner lens
beneath the spires of the great city
on the morning we arrived.

SURF CITY

On the bronzed trays in the open-air bars,
horse's head is served
and the tray-light matches the thighs
of the statue stepping topless from the sea.
A golden coin with her face in profile
crosses over in the cormorant's beak.
Mattresses float by on the water
sailed by cross-legged children
singing their sweet alouettes,
and watching the wavering gods on shore
hauling silicon into shimmering mounds.
So romantic, these midsummer days:
the jug-bearing servants embossed
on the cool sarcophagi of the CFOs,
a huge faint moon in a blueberry sky,
the seasonal waters in which one can flush
his scalp and beard of all ash and dust
from the great libraries of the past.
To hear the cry of Merlin
from the bath house is a thrill.
To see Casper disrobed and spying on bathers

from his tower of *World Books* piled in a stack!
Through the grand flume of the clouds,
a new fleet of Innisfrees takes to the sky
over the heads of the city planners,
over the balustrade to the pier,
over the infants flipped onto their backs
reading the style guide, taking its quiz.
Ah, the double-stream soda guns.
Ah, the gondolas chained to the jetty.
The horses' manes still flecked with sand,
and two girls for every boy.

GENERAL HOSPITAL

I was first on the ward
to see the sunlight fall
on the lighthouse stairs.
It kept me, emboldened,
alive for some time,
I moved more humanely,
troubling no one,
as if all distance
had been removed
as far back as childhood,
closing a gap between
boy and his overpass,
boy and his flowers beneath it.
Now in sublime vestments,
I could look at the past
and see its stream
of headlights flowering,
lit by a system of roots
to which I swore I'd attend
and promised to water,
underpass god

that I had become,
who knew the way
through the shining fields
which opened onto
a slumbering lighthouse,
and I the only remembrancer
permitted to leave
a cupful of sun in offering.

TO A FEVERISH CHILD

Again I woke up in bed with the morning fear
and again from the window I watched
a string of schoolchildren led down the street
and wished to be you: the sick and absent child
with the chime of fever in your eyes. You haven't yet
learned how to give, you can lie, grow jealous,
and hide without reprimand, and what's best,
you're asleep. You don't have much to memorize,
save for a hidden path from your school to a private tree,
or the name your mother gave you in the night:
delirious. You may have felt the terror
that comes before health, and you may have dreamt
in your fever, as I have, that all of the daylight,
street lamps, and house lights are pulled
into the reservoir while you sleep.
But at least you know relief will always wake you.
You can't conceive that at dusk I drove my car
alongside the water to get my thoughts right,
and leaned my body over the reservoir's lip
to watch my face among the neighborhood lights,

swallowed and renewed. I felt for one moment
insane and holy. What do you have to do but wait
for your mother to come down the hall with a cloth?

A VISION

Visitors to the nighttime,
hand in hand, we wept,
we dreamt in the mountains
we heard our child
down every mineshaft
making a song.
Then I was deep
in the shadows of a mine
holding the brain
of an owl in my hands.
You had to carry me
in your arms
through the valley
to where the tigress wore
her silver bridle.
In her mouth was a basket.
In the basket,
the pale, young bodies.
None were ours.
Her golden eyes closed
on our grief.

A river appeared.
The boatsman arrived.
I woke to the cry of a bird
forcing its body
through the thatching
of our roof.
You were outside
driving a headstone
among the sloe blossoms
into the earth.

FAMILY FARM

The grist is plentiful,
nearly loping into the stores.
It almost hovers
over the moat to market.
I pause in that lower flood
scowling into my spray gun.
Against the dusk,
our family's crest:
a plain of wheat
bent in my younger fist
shines from the side
of our silo.
I am unfeasible now
in my protective suit
and mask. Tapes
of my flushed speech
spool away from me
into the auburn,
distancing fields.
My sons have all gone
blaring into the opulent

teatimes of the Northeast.
They call me
a sample section
of a dying population,
clarified butter for a face.
In a shed, I hear
the thinning crows
stringing together
a final crown
of rebar for my head.

LITTLE LORD FAUNTLEROY

I failed to memorize the giant's face.
I failed to return with a flake from his mask.
I dropped a bottle of cinnamon Glade
down the well at the mountain's side.
In a shower stall of my old dormitory,
I slaked my thirst against the dripping wall.
I did my coursework before I was ready.
I came to, spitting up tricolored foam.
Please have a little modesty,
dangling sword on its string above me:
stop giving me that cosmological-
tea-cake-in-the-throat sensation!
Little Lord Fauntleroy's the name:
loyal customer, rewards cardholder,
and rest assured, when I'm in my tomb,
my collar will still be starched with the smoke
of the pheasant breasts served peasant-style
in our family jet scraping over the sea.
Yet I do doff my cap to the factories' runoff.
I'm on a new medication now.
I kiss all babies and persons of interest

like a feather touching the lion's singed mouth.
Excuse me while I adjust my crotch
on this off-white vinyl triclinium couch
before the first piped notes of my eclogue resound
and I am raised up high on a weightless cloud
to my second life on the good side of midtown
at Child of the Hushed Eraser school.
In its glass-display-case-lined hallowed halls,
a great American debate has begun—
whether or not one should lie about
the U-Haul mileage (how quaint, what fun!)—
and poor Calpurnia, freshman,
sulking alone in the school's herbarium:
for each of my former life's crimes, we split
a ring of cocktail shrimp in the sun.

NOYE

I am permitted to hear
the pearl on my dresser.
She speaks to me
in the parlance of pain.
I keep her
in my shallow pocket,
and sleep with her
clasped between my hands.
The wake of my boat
unravels down the byways,
and all day I pick
the white pith of my thumbs.
Sometimes the boat
is flanked by swimmers
trying to catch up.
They raise their heads to breathe,
and dip them down again.
They raise their heads to speak,
and I can see their loved ones'
precious objects
strung around their necks

on chains.

One was still teething

as he clung to an oar

while I glowered down at him.

I lift my simple,

dust-covered cinder block

over my head,

then let it fall,

then pull the body up.

We are passing through the fens.

His hair is wet.

I take his rings.

His breath flowering

timelessly behind us

in the frozen morning air.

ON QUALITY HILL

Winter staggered along with its ass
under too hard a spell for it to shake,
and the pine re-entitlement programs
had been slashed. But thinking better
of the bald white ground, each tree
returned and bent itself back into place
just nearly straight enough to give us
our natural world and as well achieve
the state order for no delirium.
I admit beneath their branches
I have once or twice allowed myself
to trust their perfectly synchronized shadows.
On the blasted heaths of our backyards,
we let them shade our families
no more than an inch or two,
and before I know it I'm coming to
in the dooryard snorting noisily,
arms deep in prizes and outsize checks.
Take, for example, the official request
to forego the sonogram, simply to hope:
it appears not one of us is distressed.

Because no one handles tears like us
with our tricked-out horse's sense
of pain. Our object is to be led
into a neater submission, blue as a god.

TENOR

Piece of quartz on your way to choir,
forehead holding the coldest sun,
no one can see you disappear your talismans:

out of your parka, into the bowl,
you relinquish a single section of fruit
from the food pyramid, your offering.

Then for an hour on felted risers,
beneath a vaulted ceiling,
you're made to sing the kyrie:

have mercy on every plane that has vanished,
mercy on every waterfall
that drops from the office mezzanines

in parts per million
onto the trees and earth and men and beasts
as equally as our mild hearts are equal.

When singing, you're told to fold your hands.
When singing, you're told to round your lips
to make the shape of a well.

In the dark of your mouth,
I know you are saving
an orb of your human spit.

Little silver thought,
you changeling, protector of the snowscape
walking the wet retaining wall to your house at dusk,

the history of your private life has begun.

REFRAIN

When you are given
a piece of black paper in school
and taught to make a cube,
you carry it home in your hand,
and though it comes home
damaged under the maples,
you learn to press it
with a strictness
against your thigh
to keep its shape
at attention by your bed.
Call it a cage
for the evening,
a cage for the pixelated dark
in which move the night's
infinite animals
who crawl on the inside
faces of your walls,
over your body,
and dance
on your twenty nail beds.

Outdoors,
in the broader shape
of the neighborhood,
larger versions shift across
the streets and lawns.
Street lamps light their haunches
as if they can only be seen
in retreat: two legs, an arm,
and a glimpse of their backs,
no faces or mouths,
like the video copies
of your small frame
you reach toward
whenever you're led beneath
a grocery store's screens.

CHILDREN OF THE EPIPENDOM

Steadfastly groomed,
with rich inner worlds,
and dressed in the high
style of the conqueror,
did they know it
to be a luxury
to shout down
into the depths
where they were devoured?
They did not.
What they saw down there
were smaller than children,
children's children,
tantamount only
to a blade of grass,
a mussel shell,
while up above
we gave them
their permanent names:
Adam Known-Torturer,
Fortune's Teen of the Year,

Tarquin Pubescens,
the Preteen *Bachelor*,
staving off
each panel of sun
from their necks
to preserve
the gorgeous skin.
What harrowing etchings
they make
on the sides
of their respirators
while they sleep,
the undressed dolls
of their eldest sisters
tucked under
their delicate arms.

BLIND MINOTAUR LED BY A CHILD

To her I must seem vulnerable
because I cannot die.

I let her guide me up the staircase,
and we do not touch a single wall.

She moves my hands
over the drawings in her notebook

and I cannot see, but graze
the words on the opposing page:

aurora borealis written backwards,
and a box which she has checked off in reverse.

My eyes are the husks of stars
and as blank as the javelin thrower's mind.

It dwarfs me now:
the chime of horseshoe players in a field,

an oven door half-opening
in the woods behind the school.

A pinecone sinks
into the mire beside the village,

a delivery boy balances two quarts
of steaming broth between his hands.

All these have withstood my unlooking.
Dog-faced leviathan,

to have languished
in my dingy, vaulted penitence,

I long to reemerge
like the figurehead of a ship

into the blue of the fire's spectrum,
into the perfect sight of the bird.

CENTAURS IN THE TURNPIKE WOODS

They speed away
in their rental cars at night,
leaving the woods bare
and crackling
with their discharge.
I have seen the centaurs
using the light from their phones
to shave among the scrub pine.
If they hear the touch
of a hand on a windowsill,
they will zip up
their toiletry bags
and cower back
to their champagne-
colored sedans.
They are difficult to see
in their navy blue suits
as they shift
through the trees.
And the earth sips,

when no one is watching,
the foam from the mouthwash
and lather they leave
in the dark with the flowers.

HUMAN WATER

Boy beside a rain barrel
curling his hand
over its edge.

His fingers yellow
in the roof-dark water
he can't see.

He places on its surface
a branch of holly
from the yard,

and its reflection
breaks his own.
I'm remembering,

and misremembering,
and stepping through
a public field.

43

I am alone,
so there are three of us.
Within my body,

there is also me
but more corrective,
age-rings in my eyes,

coming down from the house
to stay him, shouting:
What did I tell you

about playing with visions
by the water
when I'm not watching?

His small hand raises
a wasp, a lamp, a deer, a field,
a wall, a flame,

calling for anything he names
to be lifted over
the barrel's edge.

RATIONS

Fawn, asp, or crow,
my hand is lingering
over its choices
placed in a row
before my little fire.
The plot of this earth
is squirming.
The trees are locked
with a master key
in the dark.
Can they smell me
from here,
tireless cook
and my smoke rings
at dawn, the bib
of a much younger
man at my chest,
these poor people
wearing the color
of cinders? Here
they come running

down through
the cul-de-sacs,
carriages for the dew.
Surely I have made
something worthy
of a late empire.

FROM THE OVERFLOW HOTEL

To purchase a little land,
to take a little shut-eye
beneath the friezes of the state,
to learn the position of the heavens
inlaid on the ceilings
of our country's Westins, yes,
it is a substantial day
for toweling off
a courtyard statue in the sun.
At quitting time,
I press my forehead
to the hallway's ice machine,
and see a blood-red curtain
draped across a field,
and the vast epidemic
of the soldiery overstepping
what an ugly year it was
for marching us out
to the bluffs to face their god,
though we did look
preternaturally beautiful

in our uniforms
like a somnolent hand
holding a violet to its nose.
And each morning woken
by the pole of the super,
each morning sprung
at the drill of the whistle
out of my hibernaculum,
indelibly bound to my mission
to swiff the garbage
from the fountains,
to reset the scoreboards,
to polish the skywalk,
to shoo the R&D children away
from pissing out over
the tremulous vistas,
and each night in my sleep mask
atop the bedspread's flowered maze,
I wait to hear the rippling
of the elk in the ravine below.
He is carefully rinsing off
his family's Pyrex in the flood,
his song as old as woe.

CENTRAL CASTING

He answered the call for Pale Christ With a Nordic Touch.

I was reading for His Jailor With the Hundred Eyes.

In the emptied banquet hall, I opened the accused's mouth wide.

Released his frozen burst of flavor crystals to the air.

Seawater dampened the inner lining of his diadem.

How did he find his way to central casting,

hauling his triple-glass cross atop his shoulders,

scanning the road for traffic before the overflow hotel?

Born as he was in his mother's esophagus,

chewing shards of her childhood's globe in its dark

while she waited in line at the adult-sized chessboard,

a young, green corn husk like a garland in her hair.

Or a flower on a distant wave.

A boatsman ferrying the jailor toward it.

He who would hunt them, mother and child.

He who would eat them beneath his curtain of blood.

The prow of the boat as it reached her body:

the shape of a pyramid mounting Snow White.

HEAD IN THE ORCHARD

Why the boatsman spared me I do not know.
He stood above me on the overpass
without a word, his eyes downcast and clear,
his wreath of sawgrass hung around his neck.
This in the time of the orchard full of fruit.
I looked at him, a worm within my feasting,
squinting through the scouring light,
and while we did not break our stares,
my blind hand shook behind me as I searched
my satchel for the axe. I freed its knot
and smelled the outbreath of the sap
and sunlight on the blade within
then cinched the cord again, that scent
now wasted on the world. I spared him too.
Half my life I'd spent sleeping in the sun,
the other under the orchard's starlight,
the roseate sun to seek. Here is the tree
to which I nailed my head, and northward,
the flattened field where I loosed my dogs,
my body borne behind them making tracks

the boatsman could not read atop his ledge,
although I know he did look down at me
once more, his forehead softened, hair salt-damp,
his bone-white cape whipping downwind.

STUDY FOR THE BOATSMAN

Single tenant
of his emptied city,
coat blown open,

he carries a bucket
of quicklime
to the coast.

The birds make
their derisive whistles,
watching from the woods.

On a sun-bleached
colonnade at dusk,
he leans against a pillar
drinking discontinued colas.

The frieze behind his head:
children eaten by a fish.
It's chiseled into stone.

He must have seen to it
himself, must have studied it
with approbation,
limestone in his hair.

In his whirlpool, later,
he presents himself
a single darkened plum.

Watch the warping
of his face
in its reflection,

its flesh swallowed gratefully,
the pink stone spit
into the garden below.

Former master of the *Dove*,
head bent to his chest
and water beading in his hair,

he sleeps in his bath,
then wakes at dawn
to heft the refuse
from the tidal pools:

slabs of viaduct and filigree,
half skeletons of ruminants.
His eyes eager and wild

and wavering
like the honeycombs
at the edge of his very vast forest.

GERYON

I throw the end of the cord
over the edge of the world
into sleep. The other end tied
to my waist. The teacher
is faintly speaking: "Soon
you'll be calmed by a truth
you'll believe you designed
yourself." The cord whips
down into the whirlpools
beneath us and hauls up
what has been planned:
a shape with my face rises,
an arced, hokum figure
bending its torso, bowing to me
in the spring sunshine
and the spray. I wake alone
among trees, the shelving units,
the municipal waste.
It is noon, and half of my life
is over. Before me, the ragged
upward mass of the foothills.

FLUDDE

The light had its gradient pull.
I scanned away from the schoolyard
with the lens sparkling. And the moon
divvied up into separate grains.
I find the coin I'd skimmed
from the lake, and when it cries,
I'm reminded: the lead ocean itself
is waiting with love within us.
None of us dared trim away
the snake's skin that summer for fear
of what was beneath its unwinding.
Beyond us, all of our glassware
is being sown over in a future
where a shoulder blade is found
and dug up again. It will know
nothing of us, or the ocean
that crept through the sun. Difficult
child, shrilling lake unhinged,
you stand in a state of mild yawning
in a church of your own gold,
peeling your shadow from

the diving board. *On stage!*
it was said. *File in!* The sounds
of undressing and song coursed through
the back halls, then were lost behind
the beverage machines. We were placed
in line as if meant to return
our crossbows. And I loved these
cross-purposes. At night,
in our beds, our legs snapped like dawn
on a hinterland of ice.
We were told God was winnowing us
into fascinating lutes.
While the flood ranged southward.

SWIM CLUB KATE IN THE CITY OF DIS

The devils studied her spit
for its secrets,
but found she knew nothing,
discovering only
a sugar cube road to Damascus,
a desert of felt,
and a pyramid built out of foam.
And these, they knew,
were merely a fourth grader's
knowledge of God,
so they let each droplet
fall from their mouths
and onto her swimsuit
and turquoise-polished toes.
And they mind-read
her bike lock combination,
and looked beneath
her bright pink visor
while the mimicking birds
on the high pylons
pronounced her medications'

names all wrong,
and a threadbare towel
curled into itself
in the plastic bag
that spun on her wrist,
and they sent her down
to a lower pool,
and she joined the crowd
in Bermuda shorts,
which had formed to watch
a set of twins
who were fed by the devils
while treading water,
and they watched and rewatched
a sunburned girl
who had to repeat
her death by drowning,
and had to receive
a teenage boy lifeguard's
hair in her mouth
while he tried to save her,
his aluminum whistle
grazing her cheek.
Then a door in a sea-mural wall slid back
and the little jackal god appeared
with his shriveled penis
and his black Lycra loincloth
to carry the girl away,

and the masses shuddered
when his hoofbeats fled.
It was then the Sea God spoke aloud:

> *Test Kate now for her vanity!*

It was spoken by him
who can only be seen
from the bottom of the diving well,
who is one fluorescent circular eye
with thousands of naked frog-kicking lashes.
Before him Kate swam the crawl,
the backward crawl,
and the breast unashamed,
and was asked by the God:

> *Now can you swear*
> *you will cease to expectorate,*
> *to come unshowered,*
> *to bring us your scabs?*

And Kate nodded to him
with some dignity,
an orange soda still ringing her lips,
and she held out the plastic bag
tied to her wrist
and he gave her the flakes
from a diving mask
and one hundred threads
from his finest suit,
and said she must braid them
piece by piece

into the map she would use
and on which she would sail
should she ever wish to return.

BOY ROWING ASLEEP

Yes I believed in the boats
in their frantic and nongeometrical wavering
but I was forced to resist their diffusion
the boatsman draining the rain from his gloves
his hair untidy and streaming all over the prow
so I hauled the cord of my fever
from stairwell to stairwell into the tower
and only spied its blurry hall of fossils
through tears. Once in the deciduous forests
we laid our trading cards down on a cover of leaves
and we rose in the summer corn
to pull a dish from a fragrant fire.
This was before the floes
before the maze of sleep
and learning to make the compass-shape
in bed with our hands. Yes I believed in the boats
but I was willed to life in this tall citadel
where I sat in soot like a rose beneath glass
and nightly asleep in my unswept space
I rescued myself, sent a braid of my hair
through the keyhole and followed it

down to the banks and into the seat
of my waiting skiff, the tin of its oarlocks
shivering, and I bandied with the clueless stars
the madrigal singers were fording the rivers in gowns
and I toasted to a totalness and so fled the ministry alone.

LANDSCAPE

Beside the harbor,

beside its sea,

beside its snow

that dissolves

when it falls

onto the surface

of its sea,

you can hear

the municipal waste

as it gathers

in the woods:

the siennas, alizarins,

and cornelians of trash

amassing there

among the snow

and pines.

The waste blows loose

into the harbor,

and it carries snow

onto the sea:

luminaries

for a silver age,
preemptive peace.
And snow falls
onto the face of a child
who stands beside
about to open his mouth.
Out comes the rattle
of silverware
washed in a sink:
music you heard
from a window
you stood beneath
in a courtyard
when you were small.

DEMOLITION

For a week, a detour takes me
past the windows of an Econo Lodge.
I invent what's on the other side
each morning, beginning
with what I know is there:
an absent clerk, an empty lobby,
some dark green carpet
joined in places with duct tape.
I add a chair for myself to sit in
and make the smaller arrangements:
a door to a bedroom
closed just enough
to hide a figure inside,
open enough to reveal a bed
that looks like a gurney,
a wrist lying face up
on the sterile and steamed
white sheets. What am I
intending to have happen here?
Hard to tell if it's my wrist

or someone else's that's meant
to emerge from that room.
I'm getting a feel for the lobby though:
within days I learn to fix a sugar drink
from sweetener packets and sink water.
I place a Styrofoam cupful
in front of the bedroom door
and watch for movement.
But by the end of the week,
the detour signs are pulled,
and my car is directed
back to the highway,
granting me another view:
the demolished building
the city was shielding me from.
A crane now sifts through fragments
and debris, sorting them
into one pile or another.
As it holds each piece of metal in the air
to let it flicker for a moment,
for me it is lifting the door,
the bed, the sheets, the wrist,
and the cup that now is filling

with an early sunlight on the floor
of the motel. I watch in the mirror
as each object hangs, then drops.
My car approaches my building and work.

I walk the sea-foam hallways

to my desk, and when the people that I pass

say, *Morning*, I say, *Morning*, too.

I can't be certain who is waking whom.

HARUSPEX

The office lights chose
to remain half lit
for the rest of the fall.
I went whistling
the song of two crows
down a hall unknowingly.
Through my phone,
an exam room
slipped into my ear
and unfolded
its expanses brightly.
How does one get to sleep
in a city of snowfields?
My father sent me
an absentee ballot
and asked, did I think
my future was secure?
I daydreamt throughout,
and my eyes flew doubly
over a man on a raft
downriver: his body thin,

his liver a white star
pressed against his skin.
It asked me to extract it
for its portents.
Back in the office,
my Xeroxes spilled
from a seam of light.
They handed me
a memory of warmth
from distant fires.

OVERALL MESSAGE

Here come seven-year-old toughs
with chunks of condemned buildings
carried in front of their faces.
The company fleeces hang
in the indoor driving range break room
with feverish openness.
The course pro comments mildly
on the male torso, its pallor and grace.
The vice-chair at the boardroom table
is scraping a laxative in his lap
to the size of an aspirin,
and his lover waits in his penthouse
using her pink can of pepper spray
to strike the keys of a xylophone
into his voicemail to let him know
she's in the city. I leave the meeting early.
Truant children on the staircase
crop a photo of me till they have my face.
In the lounge next door,
they're revising the phrase *good times*,
so I go in and get the print version

slid to me under my placemat
then leave with the restaurateur
to pack our things. It's been a long trip,
a long year, a long downturn toward here.
Behind our backs, the waiters begin
the slideshow of our blighted mansions,
and all of their patrons' heads
hunch forward into their ledgers,
baby blue lanyards dangling from their necks
which read: *Cities of Concern.*
And the willow trees are praying for us.
And they shame us with their reverence
and cool discretion. "Poison is poison!"
a nurse-in-training scolds a child
on the curb in front of us.
"Don't let me catch you in the cabinet again!"
In the entryway to the hospital,
their godhead is leaning peacefully.
At its feet, someone's half sister places
a handful of Swedish Fish, wet with her saliva.
I begin my new organization here.

PERIPHERY

You are evading me.
You are just beyond me.
You are the length
of the hood of a car
away from me,
and thinner
than I remember,
dressed as if undressed
after work.
I reach until
I can meet your hand.
But you are in front of me
like the moon
on one week,
then behind me
like the moon on another.
You are trying to move
toward the doors of a church
we both know
and I won't let you.
I step in front

and you step to the side
saying, *Stay on the periphery*
and we'll be in touch
this summer.
But what's here
that won't let me speak to you,
that keeps me
from letting you go inside,
that makes you
want to go inside?
Once two friends
stood on opposite banks
of a stream.
Then they were men
and a river,
and then two ghosts:
the story becoming
more distant and strange
the more I fear
the person listening.

THE WOODSMAN'S RING

I saw you once when you were young
leaning against the pearl-lined cistern on the hill
whittling a streak of quartz with a small knife
the stain of palm wine on your chin
the gleam of a brass ring on your finger
in the shape of a crocodile
which floated all its life on the river
at the hands of gods and mortals
sometimes a boy sailing its back to shore
sometimes a preacher with the hair of a girl
in the pocket of his buttoned vest.
Now you suck your ring hand in the dark
and wait for death to sidle up beside your fire
riding to you on the back of a child
with cat's-eye marbles for his eyes.
Death, her eyes are pleurisied.
Death, she favors the wounds of her child
and so no longer strikes him.
And when she finds you, she parts your hair
and with her two-pronged tongue
she bathes you, and bathing you

tastes sugar, cherries, and the alimentum
on which you were fed when you ran on two legs
through the sandwoods with courage and ruth.

MOUNT AIRY RESORT AND CASINO

There is no longer a path
to Mount Airy Resort and Casino.
It is covered in ice, and mist conceals
its controversial shuttle system.
Overturn a stone at the head of the path,
and you will find a heartwarmed citizen
clutching his prize of an emerald-encrusted
kitchen appliance, staring upward
as if your eyes are a second showroom
he can enter. These company men underfoot,
travel-sized lotions and handwashes
filling the pockets of their coats.

Come sit with me overnight on Mount Airy
and watch the general admission line up
to see the tyrant in the valley below
headlining his big-name venues
doing "Sumer Is Icumen In."
I admit I do still envy the children
when, wreathed in flowers, he passes by
on a glacier carved in the shape of his face
throwing tokens carved in the shape of his face.

When I was a child of the valley
I was a garden unto myself.
I cut it down with my teeth
and ate its fruit, the skin of my thumbs,
and I thought for this I heard my name
cheered loudly into the spaciousness,
the suspension bridges and overpasses
transferring their powers to me.

But now not even the color of things
can bring me pleasure here:
not the paling infinity pools,
not the final blue shouts from the waterfalls,
not the complimentary daycare center
with doors painted shut in aquamarine.

Each spring my brother returns
to visit me from Presque Isle.
Worm of a man, he married young:
a dour club-version of "Greensleeves"
played without soul. Small wonder
we parted ways while our hair was still dark,
while he bottled and vialed the wave pool's waters
and called from the peaks to the show choir boys
on the interstate in their hotel robes.
They too are vanished into the fog
or asleep at the bottom of the artificial lakes,
their tour buses docked and overwhelmed
in the loneliness of the cinnamon trees.

At dusk, sunlight departs from the mountain
and pulls away from the shoulder pads
and little anchors on the gilded buttons
of my navy blue evening wear.
I rend, I cry. I can't stop touching my waistline
or playing video baccarat in my head.
Should you wish to know the moral of my story,
let the boy scouts tell you the one about the child
who died at the nondenominational summer camp
in a cage of ice. Then come find me
at Mount Airy Resort and Casino.
I will show you his mask of museum-grade wax
that I carefully place over mine.

ASTROLABE

Standing atop the moon,
I aim my tractor wheel at the Earth.

Freezing-cold disc in my hands,
it believes in an unconditional love.

It misses the sound
of the axe against the tree,

the pill dividers opening calmly
and translucent green.

Its child's-errand was always
to detect itself in the water,

to rest in a clean white bed
that unfolded from the wall.

Now I draw it closer to my face.
Now my eye's blue flame.

Through the icy axles,
I measure the distance home.

LITTLE TOM DACRE IN HEAVEN

And through my tears
in the hereafter,
I see my tears received below
on the arched back
of a chief of staff
dragging his skiff behind him
and wandering
the incorporated limits
in his suit the color
of underground lakes.
Lo, to feel as indifferent now
as the candy dispenser,
the unlit carport,
the blue flag sunk
in front of my old
elementary school,
but here too
I can touch my heart
to a knotted tree
and its murmuring
can be heard in the leaves

of an office plant
misted down on earth
by a man committing
lines of love to memory
in his green security jacket.
Child I was
who once sought guidance
at the whirlpool,
the colored milk
still in my bowl,
who was lifted
for inspection by command,
and when I was held
in the doctor's arms,
his ears were warm with blood
and I shielded my mouth
with a tear-shaped mint,
a spell to halt
the interrogating lamp
as he spun it
toward my face.
It was well-covering time.
We children were served
our salad greens
in centurion's helmets
never to be worn again.
And the widow Bilgewater
was taking down our names

while we gathered and carried

the covering-sticks,

her eyes as blank

as the backside

of the board of health

and the dark pools of rain

that gathered there,

and in them I saw:

    the sleepers covering the hills with their bodies

    a whalebone wrested from the tabernacle by thieves

    a furniture outlet looted clean

    a woodsman glancing over his shoulder

    as he bit into a greasy heart

    the piles of ash in the wilderness

    the stinking ligatures on the helmsman's neck

    a sea full of in-flight magazines

    a band of actuaries discarding their ties

    to bark at the brown water stain of the moon

until the mesh hood

was pulled down

over my naked head,

and I woke up here.

NOTES

The collection's title is derived from *Noye's Fludde* (Noah's Flood), twentieth-century British composer Benjamin Britten's short opera for amateur players, which includes children who are cast as the ark's animals. I performed in this play as a boy.

"Blind Minotaur Led by A Child" takes its title from, and is inspired by, a 1934 etching by Pablo Picasso titled *Minotaure aveugle guidé par une fillette dans la nuit* (Blind minotaur led by a little girl through the night).

Both the title of the poem "Surf City" and its line "and two girls for every boy" come from the popular song "Surf City" written by Brian Wilson and Jan Berry.

"Mount Airy Resort and Casino" was inspired by the work of Cold Mountain poet Hanshan.

The title of the poem "Human Water" is derived from a line from Gaston Bachelard's *The Poetics of Reverie*: "Childhood is a human water, a water which comes out of the shadows."

"Little Lord Fauntleroy": Originating in Frances Hodgson Burnett's nineteenth-century children's novel of the same name, Little Lord Fauntleroy became the archetype for the impoverished child of secretly noble heritage, characterized by his ostentatious Little Lord Fauntleroy suit.

"Little Tom Dacre in Heaven": Little Tom Dacre is the boy who has a vision of freedom from the exploitation of child labor in William Blake's "The Chimney Sweeper."

ACKNOWLEDGMENTS

Grateful acknowledgment is made to the editors and staff of the following publications in which poems from this collection initially appeared: *Bear Review, Best New Poets, Blackbox Manifold, Conjunctions, diode, Drunken Boat, Gulf Coast, Horsethief, Huck Magazine, Ladowich, The Literary Review, Matter, New Ohio Review, Numéro Cinq, Open Letters Monthly, Oversound, Poet's Country, Poetry Daily, Prelude, Prodigal, Public Pool, Salt Hill, Sixfold, Syracuse.com,* and *The Winter Anthology.*

Thank you, Dean Young. Thank you, Sarah Gorham, Jeffrey Skinner, Kristen Radtke, Ariel Lewiton, Kristen Miller, Danika Isdahl, Joanna Englert, and all at Sarabande Books for your generosity, help, and insight.

JENNIFER WETZEL

PETER MISHLER was born in New Jersey, and lives in Kansas City where he teaches and serves as an editor for *Drunken Boat*. His work has been featured at *Conjunctions*, *The Literary Review*, *Public Pool*, and *Poetry Daily*, and was selected for the *Best New Poets* series. This is his first book.

SARABANDE BOOKS is a nonprofit literary press located in Louisville, KY. Founded in 1994 to champion poetry, short fiction, and essay, we are committed to creating lasting editions that honor exceptional writing. For more information, please visit sarabandebooks.org.